PIER 21

GATEWAY OF HOPE

LINDA GRANFIELD

TUNDRA BOOKS

Published in Canada by Tundra Books, *McClelland & Stewart Young Readers*,
481 University Avenue, Toronto, Ontario M5G 2E9

Published in the United States by Tundra Books of Northern New York,
P.O. Box 1030, Plattsburgh, New York 12901

Library of Congress Catalog Number: 99-75869

Canadian Cataloguing in Publication Data

Granfield, Linda
    Pier 21: gateway of hope

1st ed.
ISBN 0-88776-517-3

I. Ports of entry – Nova Scotia – Halifax – History – Juvenile literature.
2. Canada – Emigration and immigration – History – 20th century – Juvenile
literature. 3. Immigrants – Canada – History – Juvenile literature. I. Title.

JV7225.G72 2000   j325.71   C99-932782-8

We acknowledge the support of the Canada Council for the Arts and the Ontario
Arts Council for our publishing program.

We acknowledge the financial support of the Government of Canada through
the Book Publishing Industry Development Program for our publishing activities.

Design by K.T. Njo

Printed and bound in Canada

1 2 3 4 5 6   05 04 03 02 01 00

A harbor, even if it is a little harbor, is a good thing,
since adventures come into it as well as go out,
and the life in it grows strong, because it takes something
from the world and has something to give in return.

SARAH ORNE JEWETT
(1849-1909)

For all those who entered Halifax Harbour to begin,
or continue, a life of adventure.

Listen.

Since 1928 we have spilled from westbound ships,
Entering the harbour as the morning mists lifted.
In joy, we shifted to one side of the deck,
Daring to tip ourselves
Onto the waiting shore.
Into Pier 21.
Into a dusty warehouse fast-filled with hopeful souls.
Into Canada.

Listen to our tired voices.
Hear our shuffling feet and murmured prayers
Of thanks as our voyage continues
On the tracks and highways,
On the way across Canada
To our homes away from war.
Away from pain and fear.
Foreign adventures have come with us.
Canadian adventures begin.
We have arrived at Pier 21.
We have stories to tell.

Listen.

Before Pier 21 opened as an immigration facility in 1928, European immigrants landed at other Halifax piers and other Canadian ports, such as Quebec City and Montreal.

Many of the early immigrants fled the crowded inner-city conditions of places like London, England, to begin new lives as homesteaders in the wide-open spaces of Canada's West. The Canadian government encouraged immigration by sending pamphlets and posters that promised free land and a climate that was "the healthiest in the world."

Who was she? What brought her to Canada? This unidentified young girl, perhaps an orphan, came early in the 1900s to begin a new life. Did she succeed?

Home children, so-called because they were sponsored by Dr. Barnardo's homes for orphaned and destitute children, travelled from England to become part of Canadian families. All too often, however, they arrived to be mistreated workers on farms and in factories.

Families large and small sailed across the Atlantic Ocean to Canada, bringing with them the traditions of their ancestors and the customs of their homelands. Scarves and shawls are tied and wrapped in different ways, long skirts are decorated with bands of colourful trim, and babies snuggle close to tired-faced mothers. The long voyage across the sea is over – long years of work await them all.

These two families were photographed on the same train platform. (Notice the wooden struts over their heads.) One father (above), wearing a soldier's uniform, clutches his immigration papers and tickets.

Six children, and perhaps another on the way, stand ready to board a "colonist train." Once again, Father holds the important family papers.

With the gentle touch of her hand, this young immigrant mother comforts her small son. The rough terrain and the bit of twig roof nearby are reminders of the vast difference between the Austria she left and the Alberta she met.

From Austria to Alberta

It often took a week or more to cross the Atlantic on huge ships. For many, it was the most important trip of their lives, and countless children grew up to tell their own children the stories of shipboard life. Dolphins swam alongside the ships. Scavenging birds followed to greedily gulp the garbage dumped in the wake each day. Young lovers nestled in the covered lifeboats. Many passengers clung to the railings or spent much of the voyage in bed as they battled seasickness.

The monotony of life on board was relieved by entertainment supplied by other passengers. Here, two young pipers use a bench as a stage and play to a chilled audience. Reading and card games also helped fill the long hours aboard ship.

This baby amuses himself with a basket of "toys," the family's passports and immigration documents.

A ship as large as the *Aquitania* could hold more than a thousand people. One English boy's mother teased him by saying that the cows that supplied the children with fresh milk each day lived behind the third funnel on the top deck!

This well-dressed family travelling from Liverpool to Halifax reminds us that not everyone emigrated because they were living in poverty in their homeland. Some moved to Canada to begin a new job or to otherwise better their family's lives. Others emigrated because of poor economic conditions, oppression, or their political views.

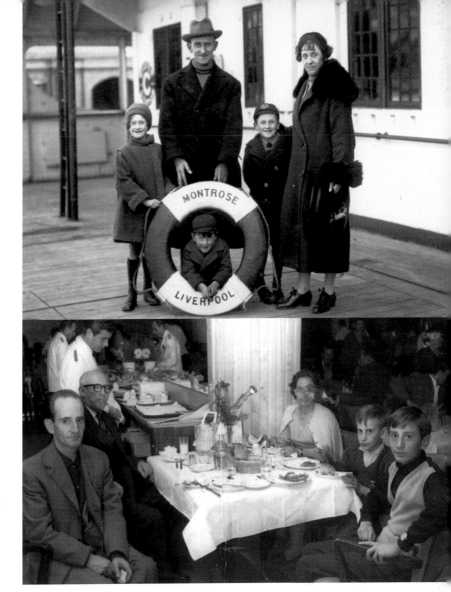

The shipboard dining room was set with white linen and china. Waiters served the many passengers at a number of sittings every meal. Special cards told you when it was your turn to eat. When a family travelled on separate men's and women's decks, everyone came together only at mealtimes. Some children saw grapefruits and bananas for the first time – and didn't know what they were or what to do with them.

From 1928 until 1971, when Pier 21 was closed, more than one million people passed through the building. Whether they were immigrants, refugees, or war brides, they each took part in an immigration process that remained essentially the same throughout the years after the Second World War.

In the 1930s, passengers disembarked onto the brow of Pier 21 and then through large doors into the building. The heavy trunks were moved by baggagemen to a special area where thousands of pieces were checked and sorted.

After the Second World War, passengers walked over a gangway (below left) that brought them directly into the second floor of Pier 21. Only 250 passengers at a time were brought from the ship to the assembly hall.

Small baggage was locked into wire cages while the families awaited processing. These cages were removed by the mid-1950s because they reminded many of threatening cells for prisoners.

In the assembly hall, rows of stiff wooden benches provided seating for the tired travellers. Anxiously, they waited for their names to be called. Pigeons cooed from the rafters above. Mothers sang lullabies to their babies. Cries of "I want to go home" were often heard.

CANADIAN IMMIGRATION

Volunteers served as interpreters for those newcomers who spoke little or no English. This interpreter is helping a Hungarian refugee in 1957. No matter what time a ship arrived, there were volunteers on duty to help however they could.

(CABIN CLASS)
IMMIGRATION IDENTIFICATION CARD
THIS CARD MUST BE SHOWN TO THE EXAMINING OFFICER AT PORT OF ARR

Name of passenger DE LONG

Name of ship AQUITANIA

Name appears on Return. sheet 10 line 18

Medical Examination Stamp

Landed immigrant

CANADIAN IMMIGRATION
MAR 22 1946
HALIFAX, N.S.
HJ

A family nervously watches as the immigration officer reviews their documents. Medical examinations were also given before their immigration status was approved. The sound of the rubber stamp imprinting the words "landed immigrant" was a welcome noise in a room filled with much foot-shuffling and many languages. The entire process could take a few hours.

The stickers on these trunks state "*Italia*" as the ship and "Halifax" as the destination. Metres of rope had to be undone before each trunk could be inspected, and the chests were retied before the landed immigrant could take them aboard the waiting trains.

The heavy trunks held professional tools required for work, family treasures, and items needed for basic daily living. Unfortunately, you "couldn't pack your friendships."

Halifax was not the final destination for all who came to Canada. Many continued their journey to other Canadian cities or towns. Some people did not receive landed immigrant status, and they remained at Pier 21 until they could return home on the next available ship. For instance, those with a criminal past were sent back. People who arrived ill were held in quarantine until they recovered and could continue with their families across Canada. Thousands were cared for in the Pier 21 dining room, hospital, nursery, and dormitories until it was time to leave the annex building and board the trains for their new homes.

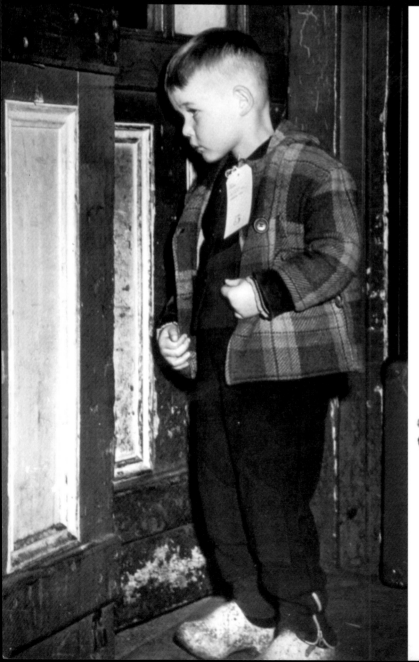

A Dutch boy peers through a doorway at Pier 21. A light-coloured train tag is tied to his coat. These tags identified both the passenger and his final destination. During the ocean voyage, passengers wore red paper tags. Such identification was no doubt useful; however, many people disliked wearing "labels" during their journey.

In the Pier 21 nursery, Red Cross volunteers changed diapers, washed and fed babies, and put them down for naps while their tired parents got some much-needed rest or took care of the family paperwork with the officials.

The city of Halifax donated fruit, cake, and candies for newcomers who arrived at Christmas. Streamers, a tree, and Santa Claus were additional pleasures at Pier 21. "I thought someone had opened a door to Heaven," recalled one boy. Holiday celebrations were also provided for the children of the Pier 21 staff and volunteers (left).

The Halifax rail yards were next to Pier 21. In fact, tracks leaving the city were located between the main building and the annex, where passengers changed their money, bought train tickets, and sent telegrams (such as the one below) either home or ahead to people who waited for them. Volunteer groups, including the Sisters of Service and the Jewish Immigrant Aid Society, helped families prepare for the tiring train trips.

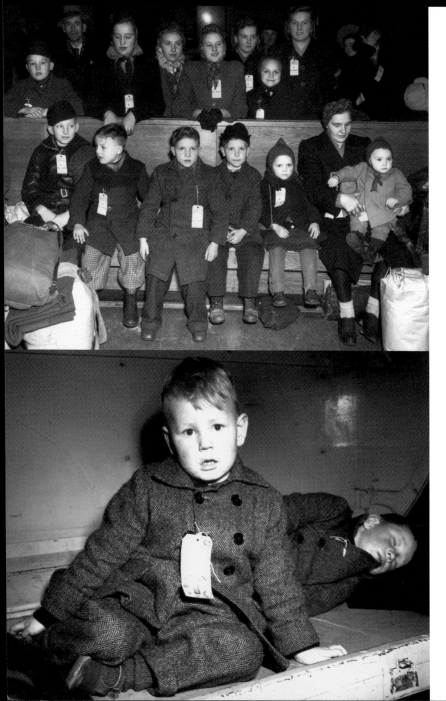

Left: **T**agged and ready, these children patiently wait to board their train coach. In the early days, people complained about the primitive conditions on the trains. There were wooden benches and stoves that spewed black soot onto everyone. It was either too hot or too cold in the coach, depending on where you were seated. Later trains had plush seats and air-cooled parlour cars.

Right: **M**any expressions fill the train windows as these children leave Pier 21 for their new homes.

These children are on a wooden sleeping platform aboard an early Canadian National Railways train. Some trains had fold-down seats that transformed into more comfortable beds. People complained about the odours of sweaty clothing and foods like tinned sardines that were brought aboard in hampers. Whenever the "colonist trains" were held on sidings while freight trains went by, passengers were glad for the chance to step out into fields for a while. The children ran among the long grasses and picked wild strawberries for an instant snack. Back on board, they settled in for a continued first look at their new country.

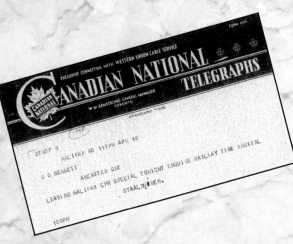

"**D**ittybags" were among the items provided to immigrants by the Pier 21 volunteers. Each drawstring cloth bag held some cigarettes, soap, jelly powder, razor blades, a toothbrush and baby bottle, and a small box of cornflakes. For many immigrants, it was the first dried cereal they'd ever seen, and they didn't always know what to do with it. Some thought it was package filler, and they shook the flakes from the box, looking for the item the flakes protected. Others came from countries where corn was chicken feed, so they didn't want to eat something meant for birds. In the immigration hall, the waiting rooms, and on the trains too, the crunch of cornflakes was felt and heard underfoot. The cereal provided many an immigrant with a story to tell, and many a Pier 21 insect with a large meal.

After Britain declared war on Germany in September 1939, hundreds of ships began moving into and out of Halifax Harbour. The bombing of Britain's cities began in 1940 and led parents to send their children out of harm's way – some to the countryside and others to Canada. About 3,000 children travelled by ship to Canada as evacuees (with their parents) and "guest children" (without their parents). Children as young as five years old came to live with relatives or complete strangers.

There was great excitement when the ships of children arrived at Pier 21. Dressed in short wool pants and caps, coats and tams, the youngsters thought they would be staying for a few months, as if on holiday. Some of them stayed longer, not seeing their parents until the war ended five years later.

Nearly identical suitcases are lined up in the baggage area as the guest children spend their first day in Canada.

A quick scrub and then it's time for lunch, complete with white bread and dishes of ice cream, items not often enjoyed in wartime Britain.

Since parents and friends were left behind, the children who visited Canada during the Second World War often brought along a special toy as a reminder of home and as something to snuggle with at bedtime.

Above left: **T**his bear's almost as large as his two British buddies. Judging by the many photographs of them, bears were the items most often selected to accompany their owners across the sea.

Above right: **I**t's "thumb's up" as the children crowd the trains that will take them to their temporary homes in every Canadian province. Some children arrived looking for cowboys in Halifax.

Right: **P**lenty of "babies" to cuddle here, and a box of Tootsie Toys to take to his new home away from home.

No dolls or stuffed teddies for this dapper young man. He has arrived with his tags, suitcase, and a set of golf clubs.

Thousands of Canadian men and women joined the various branches of military service during the Second World War (1939–45), and Pier 21 was for some their last glimpse of home. After months of training, troops embarked from Halifax for service in England and Europe. Uniforms were seen everywhere – on the streets, in the shops, at the pier. Provisions and weapons were loaded onto the ships, and troops bid their final farewells.

The Canadian artist Robert W. Chambers displayed many wartime elements in this drawing: planes, ships, jeeps, and Halifax streets filled with uniformed men and women. (Notice the kilted soldier.)

Above right: Canadian troops did not enjoy the pleasures of the pre-war stateroom. A two-berth room like the one above was stripped and converted to hold ten times that many men in "standee bunks," lengths of canvas slung between two poles.

Below right: Luxury ocean liners wore their "wartime livery," the drab grey or green paint that served as camouflage to protect the ships from enemy attacks at sea. Here, the *Aquitania* wears her battledress.

Troop ships did not always leave Halifax according to plan. During the winter months, the rough Atlantic seas could influence their departure times. The secrecy required to keep troop movements unknown to the enemy (whose submarines lurked outside Halifax) also caused departure dates to change at a moment's notice.

During the night, troops were delivered by smaller boats to ships moored in Bedford Basin, and the convoy quietly sailed out of the harbour. In the morning, Haligonians awoke to find the basin empty. Soon, more troops were transported to more ships, and so it continued throughout the war.

Canadian troops travelled from Pier 21 to various ports in Iceland and Britain. After further training periods, the soldiers, airmen, and naval personnel were transported to Europe, where they faced the horror of battle and the destruction of cities like Caen, France.

A listing of the transport ships and their dates illustrates the vast numbers involved. Thousands of men were aboard each ship, whether eastbound to Europe or returning westbound after the war. It took an average of fourteen days to cross the ocean, zig-zagging to avoid being caught by enemy U-boats.

Type of Sailing	Ship	Date
Eastbound Personnel	AUSONIA	1941/06/19
Eastbound Personnel	MALOJA	1941/06/20
Eastbound Personnel	ANDES	1941/06/21
Eastbound Personnel	BRITANNIC	1941/06/21
Eastbound Personnel	STERLING CASTLE	1941/06/21
Eastbound Personnel	PASTEUR	1941/06/21
Eastbound Personnel	WINDSOR CASTLE	1941/06/21
Eastbound Personnel	INDRAPOERA	1941/06/21
Eastbound Personnel	PASTEUR	1941/06/21
Westbound Personnel	HMS CALIFORNIA	1941/06/25
Westbound Personnel	HMS BULOLO	1941/06/25
Westbound Personnel	HMS AURANIA	1941/06/26
Westbound Personnel	HMS DERBYSHIRE	1941/06/28
Westbound Personnel	HMS CHESHIRE	1941/06/29
Eastbound Personnel	CALIFORNIA	1941/06/30
Westbound Personnel	MALDA	1941/06/30
Westbound Personnel	BALTROVER	1941/07/02
Westbound Personnel	RANPURA	1941/07/05
Eastbound Personnel	CIRCASSIA	1941/07/06
Eastbound Personnel	AURANIA	1941/07/10
Westbound Personnel	CHITRAL	1941/07/11
Westbound Personnel	HMS WOLFE	1941/07/12

WELCOME HOME!

At the end of the war, jubilant troops returned to Canada aboard the very same ships that had carried them away. The return trips took as few as four days. As the ships sailed into Halifax Harbour, fireboats escorted them. Slowly, they passed McNabs Island and the lighthouse of Georges Island. Finally, after long years of fighting, the troops arrived at Pier 21. Wounded soldiers were examined and treated before returning to their homes. As always, Pier 21 volunteers were available to help in any way.

On a summer's day in 1945, young David Campbell and his mother visited an aunt who lived near the harbour. They heard a band playing, horns and whistles blowing, and crowds cheering from Pier 21. David and his mother wandered down the hill to the pier to investigate. They walked out into the sunshine on the brow. There, looming high above the boy, was the huge *Ile de France*. Thousands of faces grinned from ear to ear and happily yelled to the people below.

Caught up in the excitement, David waved his small flag. His mother, Flora, like others standing on the brow, stooped to pick up the packages of chocolate cookies and coins that the soldiers joyously tossed to them.

David and Flora Campbell didn't know anyone returning on that ship, but like many others who crowded Pier 21 when troop ships came home, they welcomed the men and women back to Canada as if they were members of their personal family.

In 1945, the *Samaria* and the *Ile de France* pull alongside Pier 21, their decks brimming over with excited troops. Home at last!

During the Second World War, nearly one in ten Canadian servicemen married while overseas. When the war was over, their "war brides" travelled to Canada to rejoin their husbands. Clutching the hands of their small children, these women boarded the ships not knowing what they would find in Canada. Some left English city life for a future on a Saskatchewan farm. Some gave birth to babies while at sea. Some had never seen their husbands in civilian clothes and didn't recognize them. No matter how wonderful a woman's new life was, she could usually say that all of a sudden she'd "get a sore heart" when she thought of what and whom she'd left behind.

And so it begins . . . A guard of honour stands at attention as a Canadian soldier, William Sharlow, and his bride, Jean, leave an English church.

The Canadian Travel Certificate ensured the "wives, widows and children of members of the Canadian Forces Overseas" free passage to Canada. Marriage to a Canadian meant the women (and the children) automatically were considered citizens.

TO EXAMINING OFFICIALS:

THE BEARER

MRS LUCY DELONG

is travelling to Canada under the Free Passage Scheme of the Canadian Government for the wives, widows and children of members of the Canadian Forces Overseas.

Photograph of Bearer.

Signature of Bearer.

National Registration Code.

NDA · 3509979

Names of Children (under 16 years of age) accompanying holder.

Landed Immigrant.

CANADIAN IMMIGRATION
MAR 22 1946
HALIFAX, N.S.
HJF

IMMIGRATION OFFICER (1) EXAMINED 15 MAR 1946 SOUTHAMPTON

CANADIAN TRAVEL CERTIFICATE

Nº 16412

Valid for single journey to Canada direct or via the United States of America.

Name of Holder : (20204)

MRS LUCY DELONG

Issued by authority of the High Commissioner for Canada at Canada House, London, S.W.1.

on ......SEP 8 1945......

Immigration and customs officials check the papers of British war brides as they begin their journey to Canada.

Children sailing with their mothers were often on the way to see their fathers for the first time. While seasick mothers had to cope with colicky babies and take turns caring for each other's children, the youngsters played on deck and took part in fire drills.

CUNARD WHITE STAR LIMITED

After Dining Room

First Sitting

Table No. 24

Name Yvonne Gillis

Mothers and children were assigned to eat at certain sittings in the ship's dining room (complete with curtained portholes). Red Cross workers helped with the younger children.

Some of the foods, such as spaghetti, processed cheese, and hot dogs, were items the children had never seen before.

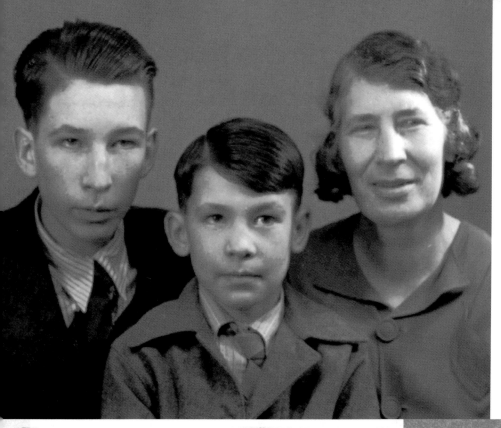

In 1946, Annie Grant arrived at Pier 21 from England with her sons Gord (centre) and Jack. Gord grew up to become a sergeant in the Metropolitan Toronto Police Force.

Below: **T**his autographed souvenir postcard is from the *Aquitania,* which is also shown docked alongside Pier 21.

POST CARD

CORRESPONDENCE.   FOR THE ADDRESS ONLY   POSTAGE

The Ship's Company of the "Aquitania" send you best wishes for your happiness and good fortune in your new life in the great Dominion, the country of your adoption.

MAY, 1946.

The Canadian war brides, just like the thousands of immigrants who arrived at Pier 21 before and after them, disembarked, were processed, and either met their husbands in Halifax or exited to the trains that would deliver them to their new provincial homes.

Canadian National Railways issued cards that reported destinations. Mrs. Gillis's new home was New Waterford, Nova Scotia. The meal coupon could be used in the train's dining car. "Dependent – Adult" means that Mrs. Gillis, not a child, will be allowed to use the coupon when ordering her meal. (A dependent is a person being sponsored by another person; in this case, a war bride is sponsored by her husband.)

The train ride, sometimes across the entire country, was an eye-opener for many of the women. Newspaper reporters snapped photographs of the women and children before they left Pier 21. Later, the women recalled some of their early reactions to the land they saw from the train windows:

> *Nova Scotia and New Brunswick were very frightening to us. We travelled through snow-covered wilderness with only the occasional wooden house throughout all the daylight hours, and . . . many of us were wondering by the time we reached Quebec, if we should be worrying about Indians still.*

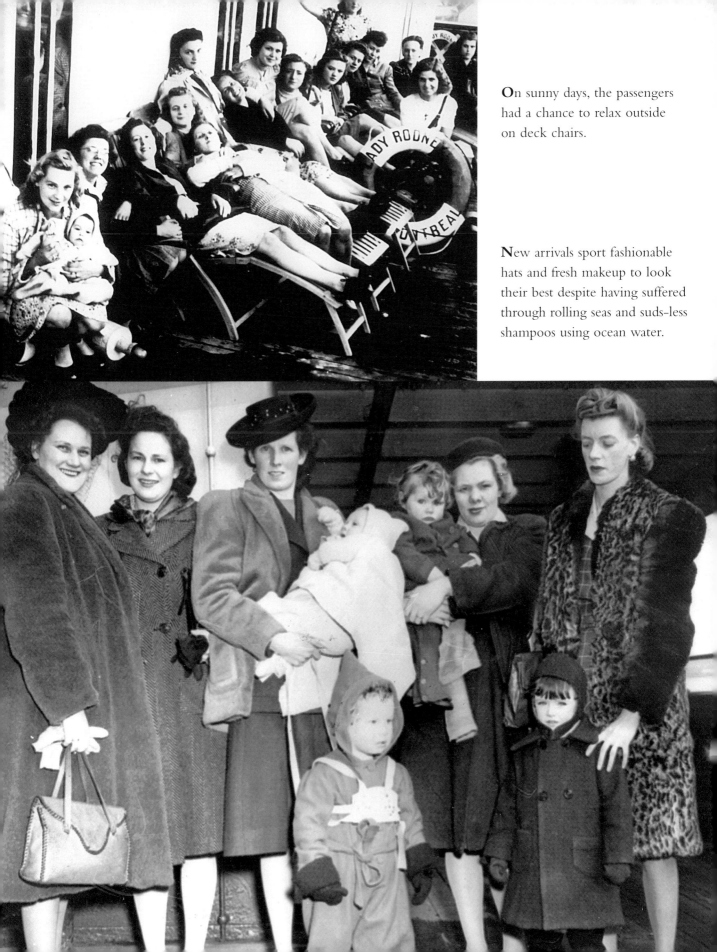

On sunny days, the passengers had a chance to relax outside on deck chairs.

New arrivals sport fashionable hats and fresh makeup to look their best despite having suffered through rolling seas and suds-less shampoos using ocean water.

After the war, thousands of Europeans came to Canada as displaced persons (DPs) or refugees. These people were escaping from invasions, oppression, or persecution in their homelands. Many left without their possessions and without time to say goodbye to loved ones. Some arrived in Canada without proper documentation or money and had to be turned away. Agencies such as the International Refugee Organization (IRO) had offices and volunteers at Pier 21 who helped many of the refugees resettle in Canada.

In the 1950s, Canada was the destination of many Hungarian refugees following revolution in their country. Here, refugees patiently wait to be interviewed before their long voyage to freedom. A teddy bear perches on some luggage, his child-owner nowhere in sight. Similar scenes could be found in Czechoslovakian cities in the 1960s as refugees fled the turmoil there.

The Levalds left their native Latvia when Russia threatened to engulf the country. They spent more than three years in DP camps in Germany, and then made their way to Canada. Mr. Levalds and his son, Ilmars, arrived in 1948 and began working on an Ontario farm. Ausma, her mother, and her elder sister were front-page news when they arrived in February 1949. Eight-year-old Ausma was chosen as the 50,000th DP to arrive in Canada. When the liner *Samaria* arrived at Pier 21, Ausma was greeted by government officials and presented with a book about Canada's birds, a doll, and a necklace, all of which she still has today. The "№ 50000" sign that Ausma Levalds holds in this photo now hangs in the resource centre at Pier 21.

These Canada-bound refugees from wartorn Italy carry their few belongings to the immigration office in Milan.

Imagine a ship built to hold forty passengers. Imagine that same ship, the *Walnut*, crossing the stormy Atlantic Ocean and arriving at Pier 21 with 347 passengers on board.

In December 1948, refugees from Estonia, Latvia, and Lithuania fled Russian armies and, with very few supplies, boarded the *Walnut*, bound for Canada. Few of the passengers arrived with proper documentation. They had no personal papers, no visas, no medical records, and no money. According to the immigration rules, most of the refugees should have been sent back to their homelands, despite the terrors that awaited them there.

Canadian officials at Pier 21, however, ignored the rules and admitted the refugees. The families were housed at Pier 21 and other Halifax locations until further arrangements for their settlement in Canada could be made. As a result of the exceptional situation of the *Walnut*'s passengers, Canadian immigration rules were changed to better meet the needs of refugees.

A little girl sleeps on her mother's lap as the *Walnut*'s passengers await processing at Pier 21.

A young man's accordion, perhaps his most valuable possession, has come across with him on the *Walnut*. Its sweet music helps the waiting refugees pass the processing time – and undoubtedly reminds them of the countries they have fled.

These pages from immigration ledgers at Pier 21 provide a lot of information about the people who came to Canada. The important "landed immigrant" stamping appears at the far right of the entry sheet.

SHEET NO. 7
THIRD CLASS

CANADIAN GOVERNMENT RETURN

S. S. TUSCANIA   SAILING FROM CHERBOURG   23RD NOVEMBER 19 38

LINE	FAMILY NAME, GIVEN NAME		RELATIONSHIP	AGE		SINGLE, MARRIED, WIDOWED OR DIVORCED	COUNTRY AND PLACE OF BIRTH	NATIONALITY (COUNTRY OF WHICH A CITIZEN OR SUBJECT)	RACE OR PEOPLE	IF IN CANADA BEFORE					WHAT LANGUAGE	
				M.	F.					BETWEEN WHAT PERIODS	AT WHAT ADDRESS	12	13	14		
1	2		3	4	5	6	7	8	9	10	11				15	
2834	BAKYG	Eleonora	sister		17	S	Czechoslovakia Oreske	Czechoslovak	Slovak	2:0	---	nil	no	yes	yes	Slovak	prepa
2836	COIFMAN	Mordko	brother	19		S	Roumania Briceni	Roumanian	Jewish		---		no	yes	yes	Jewish & Roum	prepa
2857	CONSTANTINOS	John	brother-in-law	39		M	Greece Edessa	Greek	Greek		---		no	yes	yes	Greek	self
2858	CAXCHE	Evthimia	wife		25	M	Greece Edessa	Greek	Greek		---		no	yes	yes	Greek	pre
2859	CAXCHE	Katina	daughter		1	S	Greece Edessa	Greek	Greek		---		no	yes	no	child	prep
2853	EVANOFF	Ampi	brother	25		S	Bulgaria Sofia	Bulgarian	Bulgarian		---		no	yes	yes	Bulgarian	prep
2833	KRALIKOVA	Julianna	wife		21	M	Czechoslovakia Bahy	Czechoslovak	Hungarian		---		no	yes	yes	Hungarian	prep
2831	KUCEROVA	Eliska	wife		34	M	Czechoslovakia Straznice	Czechoslovak	Czech		---		no	yes	yes	Czech	prepa
2832	KUCEROVA	Adolf	son	3		S	Czechoslovakia Straznice	Czechoslovak	Czech		---		no	yes	yes	Czech	prepa
2850	KOLBAS	Paula	wife		35	M	Yugoslavia Djurdjevo	Yugoslav	Serbian		---		no	yes	yes	Serbian	prep
2769	LE MENN	Joseph	friend	37		M	France Plouvrez de Faon	French	French		---		no	yes	yes	French	self
2677	LEPLOMB	Leopold	friend	27		M	France Doushery	French	French		---		no	yes	yes	French	qee
2735	MOLNAR	Julianna	wife		28	M	Czechoslovakia Mojon	Czechoslovak	Hungarian		---		no	yes	yes	Hungarian	prep
2856	POURNIAS	Jan	nephew	25		S	Greece Lidorikion	Greek	Greek		---		no	yes	yes	Greek	prep
2837	STOYAN	Petros	brother	36		S	Greece Boof	Greek	Greek		---		no	yes	yes	Greek	self
2831	SABO	Anna	wife		23	M	Czechoslovakia Joles	Czechoslovak	Hungarian		---		no	yes	yes	Hungarian	prep
2832	SABO	Helen	daughter		8	S	Czechoslovakia Joles	Czechoslovak	Hungarian		---		no	yes	yes	Hungarian	
2826																

CANADIAN IMMIGRATION SERVICE

ARRIVING AT _____ HALIFAX _____ 2 DEC 1928 19_____

SHEET NO. 7.

THIRD CLASS

VOL 14 PAGE 96

OCCUPATION		DESTINATION	GIVE NAME, RELATIONSHIP AND ADDRESS OF YOUR NEAREST RELATIVE IN THE COUNTRY FROM WHICH YOU CAME. IF A WIFE OR CHILDREN ARE TO FOLLOW YOU LATER TO CANADA, GIVE NAMES AND AGES	HAVE YOU OR ANY OF YOUR FAMILY EVER BEEN			PASSPORT			
WHAT TRADE OR OCCUPATION DID YOU FOLLOW IN YOUR OWN COUNTRY?	WHAT TRADE OR OCCUPATION DO YOU INTEND TO FOLLOW IN CANADA?	IF DESTINED TO RELATIVE, FRIEND OR EMPLOYER STATE WHICH AND GIVE NAME AND FULL ADDRESS. IF NOT JOINING ANY PERSON IN CANADA, GIVE THE ADDRESS IN CANADA TO WHICH YOU ARE GOING		MENTALLY DEFECTIVE	PHYSICALLY DEFECTIVE	TUBERCULAR	NUMBER, PLACE AND DATE OF ISSUE	MONEY IN POSSESSION BELONGING TO PASSENGER	TRAVELLING INLAND ON	ACTION TAKEN AND O'RL EXAMINER
18	19	20	21	22	23	24	25	26	27	28
844 domestic	136 domestic	Brother: Bakye Ludwik Opasatika Ontario	Mother: Bakye Teresia Oreske - XV Cpalo Sev Paris 254 Uh. Skalica 10/5/28	C 21-11-28						LANDED Immigrant
108 farmlabourer	121 farmlabourer	Brother: Zalman Coifman 3637 de Bullien street Montreal P.Q.	Father: Coifman 58 Briceni Roumania /46092 Bucarest 13/9/28	E 21-11-28			OH. 264315			LANDED Immigrant
115 farmlabourer	021 farmlabourer	Brother-in-law: Georges Camehe Prince Albert Sask. (only add.)	Wife: Amastasia Edessa, Macedonia Greece W.30845	Paris K2P 21-11-28						LANDED Immigrant
115 housewife	707 housewife	Husband: -do-	Father: John Manasis Edessa Greece 284 Salonica 25/11/28	D 21-11-28 Paris 5?P			OH.30846			LANDED Immigrant
003 daughter	607	Father: -do-	Grand father: -do-							LANDED Immigrant
108 farmlabourer	021 farmlabourer	Sister: Mrs Bogima Ivanoff 111 Trinity street Toronto Ontario	Mother: Maria Ivanova Ultsia 72 Sofia 61698/2101 Sofia 3/10/28	E 21-11-28 Paris			OH.359935			LANDED Immigrant
844 domestic	707	Husband: Kralik Michal 72 St. Patrick street Toronto Ontario	Father: Mokes A. Male Turovce - XVIII 481 Krupina 3/11/28	D 21-11-28 Paris K9P			OH.868450			LANDED Immigrant
844 domestic	707	Husband: Kucera Adolf R.R. N° 3 Chatham Ontario	Parents: Tomsej Josef Strasnice Zidovsk 891 Hodonin 17/10/28	Pasis K2P 21-11-28						LANDED Immigrant
115 son	607 child	Father: -do-	Parents: -do-	Czech Slot no no no 20-11-28			OH.863010			LANDED Immigrant
115 housewife	707 housewife	Husband: Mattia Kilban 45 River street Toronto Ontario	Father: Misko Linderak Djurdjevo Backa 328/433 V. Bekerek 13/11/28	D 20-11-28 Paris K2P						LANDED Immigrant
108 farmlabourer	021 farmlabourer	Friend: Mr. Dagara Herve 2089 rue Moreau Montreal P.Q.	Mrs Lebenn Le Cloitre Pleyben Finistere France III Chateaulin 12/11/28 Frs 1300	Fronce 13-11-28						LANDED Immigrant
108 farmlabourer	021 farmlabourer	Friend: Mr. Vincent Mocera 48 rue Nepoleon Montreal PQ.	Wife: Mrs Leplomb 4 24 rue de la Montagne Ste Genevieve Paris France 74235 Paris 8/11/28 Frs 4000	Paris K2P 21-11-28						LANDED Immigrant
844 domestic	707	Husband: Molnar Josef 1186 St. Urbain street Montreal P.	Father-in-law: Molnar Paul Janosovce - XVIII 116 Feledince 18/10/28	Czech Slot D 21-11-28 Paris K2P			OH.322545			LANDED Immigrant
108 farmlabourer	021 farmlabourer	Uncle: N. Zogas Malatt Mercantile Co Malatt B.C.	Mother: Mrs Stamata Fournias Lidorikien Doris Greece	B 21-11-28 Paris K9P			U.14157 11279 Athens 13/11/28			LANDED Immigrant
108 farmlabourer	021 farmlabourer	Brother: Andrea Steyan Drenches 7 Marigold street Toronto Ontario	Father: Steyan Village A.o Klisi Florina	E 21-11-28 Paris K2P			OH.366633 1399 Florina 14/11/28			LANDED Immigrant
844 domestic	707	Husband: Sabe Steve 238 Enric street Box 63 Port Colborne Ontario	Mother: Albert Andrumac Joles - XXIX 489 Rosnava 31/10/28	D 21-11-28 Paris K9P			OH.357558			LANDED Immigrant
115 daughter	607 child	Father: -do-	Grand mother: -do-	no no no D 21-11-28 Paris K2P			OH.342725			LANDED Immigrant
844 domestic	707	Husband: John Sipos P.O. Box 503 Bridgeburg Ontario	Parents: Galics Istvan Kucia - XII 270 V. Revuca 29/10/28	D 21-11-28 Paris K2P						LANDED Immigrant

In March 1971, the Canadian Immigration Service officially closed its offices at Pier 21. No longer did clanging trains carry new arrivals to distant parts of Canada to begin their new lives. Gone were the hundreds of employees and volunteers, the steaming cups of tea, the bawling babies, and the stuffed bears.

From 1971 until 1997, the ground floor of Pier 21 served as a shipping warehouse and a nautical school. Artists' studios occupied parts of the second floor.

On July 1, 1999, Pier 21 opened its doors as a National Historic Site that informs and entertains through interactive displays and virtual projections. Today, Pier 21 is the last remaining immigration shed in Canada.

In 1949, young Michel Martchenkoff, with his mother and sister, left France to begin a new life in Canada. During one shipboard dinner, the French-speaking Michel drew a picture of a pod of peas to show the waiter what he wanted to eat. On Christmas Day, the Martchenkoff family arrived at Pier 21. The many stampings on Michel's passport (below right) show the path of his voyage from France to Canada.

Michel grew up to be Michael Martchenko (right), a Canadian illustrator of more than fifty children's books, including a book about John G. Magee, Jr., the teenage writer of "High Flight," the world's most famous aviation poem. Magee (centre right), a pilot, departed for Second World War duty from Pier 21 in 1941 and died overseas.

FRANCE
PASSEPORT NANSEN

N° 16

titulaire : MARTCHENKOFF

: Michel

naissance : Carcassonne (France)

naissance : 1 août 1942

lité : origine russe

m : sans

antérieur : 155 Avenue de Normandie

tenteur du présent titre n'a pas qualité pour
un passeport français.

— OBSERVATIONS —

SIGNALEMENT

Taille :
Cheveux :
Sourcils :
Front :
Yeux :
Nez :
Bouche :
Barbe :
Menton :
Visage :
Teint :
Signes particuliers :

Accompagné de ___ (nombre) ___ enfants :

Nom	Prénoms	Date de naissance

Photographie du titulaire et, le cas
échéant, photographies des enfants qui
l'accompagnent.

Signature du titulaire.

Martchenkoff. Michel.

PAYS pour lesquels le présent titre est
délivré :

Tous Pays

Le présent titre cessera d'être valable si
le porteur pénètre à un moment quelconque
en

_____

VALABLE DU 24 février 1949
AU 24 février 1950
Sauf renouvellement.

Délivré à Versailles

Date, le 24 février 1949

Le Préfet
(signature et cachet)

Pour le Préfet
Le Directeur de la Police Générale

Prorogations de Validité

emplacement du mobile spécial	Durée de validité prorogée du ___ au ___ Cachet ___ le ___

Le Préfet
(ou le Consul de France s'il y a lieu)

emplacement du mobile spécial	Durée de validité prorogée du ___ au ___ Cachet ___ le ___

Le Préfet
(ou le Consul de France s'il y a lieu)

Visas

Reproduire dans chaque visa le nom
du détenteur du titre.

P2231

13
21 SEP 1949

13
15 OCT 1949
CANADA

CANADA
-IMMIGRANT-
Visa No. P.F. 210
Authority OTTAWA C-21657
Autorité
Valid for presentation at Canadian Port of Entry within
Valide si présenté à un port d'entrée canadien dans le
TROIS
months from date of
mois de sa délivrance
Drawn at PARIS, FRANCE
OCTOBER 15TH

Visas

chaque visa le nom

TRANSIT
SEEN at the British Embassy
(VISA SECTION), PARIS
24718

IN DIRECT TRANSIT TO CANADA
(Signed)

Visas

Reproduire dans chaque visa le n
du détenteur du titre.

SÛRETÉ
NATIONALE
16 DEC 1949

IMMIGRAT (21)
1 7 DEC 1949
LIVERPOOL

LANDED ON CONDITION
OF DIRECT TRANSIT
THROUGH UNITED KINGDOM TO
Canada

IMMIGRATION OFFICER
(7)
16 DEC 1949
NEWHAVEN

CANADA IMMIGRATION
DEC 25 1949
HALIFAX, N.S.

A Brief History

1928	Pier 21 opens.
1930s	Immigration slows because of high unemployment and the Great Depression. Some immigrants return to their homelands.
1940s	Point of embarkation for Second World War troops. Arrival of evacuee and guest children, war brides, returning troops, prisoners of war, displaced persons, and refugees.
1950	Enemy Alien Prohibition changes and German immigration begins again.
1950 to 1960s	Large numbers of Italian, Greek, Czechoslovakian, and Hungarian immigrants/refugees arrive.
1971	Immigration Service leaves Pier 21.
1999	Pier 21 opens as a National Historic Site.

Who Passed Through Pier 21?

- more than one million immigrants
- 3,000 guest children during the Second World War
- 50,000 war brides and their 22,000 children
- 100,000 refugees
- 500,000 Second World War troops

(All numbers have been rounded off.)

The Pier 21 Facilities (post-Second World War)

- up to 10 immigration officers
- 22 guards, along with nurses, doctors, kitchen staff
- a nursery, kitchens, canteens, railway ticket booths, a money exchange, a waiting room for 600 people, an infirmary, dormitories to sleep 120 people, and a detention area for 10 people

The Train Coach

In front of Pier 21, you will see a Canadian National Railways car that was donated to Pier 21 by CN. The restored car, CN40109, was built in 1937, retired in 1983, and restored at the Alberta Railway Museum using authentic colours and the CNR logo from the 1930s. Many immigrants travelled to their final Canadian destinations in coaches such as this one.

For Further Information

Please check the Pier 21 Society Web site at pier21.ns.ca.
There, you can read the stories of people who arrived in Canada during the Pier 21 years.

You can also write to the Pier 21 Society at:
　　1055 Marginal Road
　　P.O. Box 611
　　Halifax, Nova Scotia
　　B3J 2R7

Shouts of joy rise from returning soldiers.

Listen.

The assembly hall stirs again with the voices of families.
Babies cry.
The world's languages jumble and soar to the rafters.
Soft lullabies wreathe small heads.
Guests come to recall the day they landed with hope.
Some encounter the gateway to Canada for the first time.
Halifax waters swish outside with blue-green speed.
Soggy foghorns blare in the grey mists.
Seagulls call to the skies.
Teacups rattle once more.
Voices of the past and present mingle and
Echo . . .

Pier 21 whispers stories.

Listen.

Acknowledgments

Heartfelt thanks are extended by the author to Ruth M. Goldbloom, O.M., Past President of the Pier 21 Society; Erez Segal, Director of Research and Information Services, Pier 21; and Carrie-Ann Smith, Research Librarian, Pier 21, for their invaluable aid during the compilation of this book. Special thanks to Joanne Schwartz, Toronto, for her tenacity; to Dave Campbell of Dartmouth, Nova Scotia, who just happened to be there on the right day; and to the many people who shared their "Pier 21 stories" and insights. Finally, a thank-you to the Tundra Books staff: Kathy Lowinger, who well knows the Pier 21 immigrant experience, Catherine Mitchell, Lynn Paul, Sue Tate, Janice Weaver, and Kong Njo.

Photo Credits

Grateful acknowledgment is made to all those who have granted permission to reprint copyrighted and personal material. Every reasonable effort has been made to locate the copyright holders for these images. The publishers would be pleased to receive information that would allow them to rectify any omissions in future printings.

Page 4: National Archives of Canada (hereafter NAC) PA187858; *6, upper left:* author's collection; *upper middle:* author's collection; *upper right:* NAC PH 260; *lower right:* NAC C09800; *7, top:* NAC PA20907; *bottom:* NAC C34838; *8, left and right:* NAC PA10254/PA10256; *9, top:* NAC C4745; *bottom:* NAC PA29788; *10, left:* NAC C-10169; *right:* NAC CO45097; *10–11, bottom:* NAC PA139646; *11, top:* Canadian Pacific Archives NS.18393; *middle:* Pier 21 Society; *12, top:* The United Church of Canada/Victoria University Archives, Toronto 86.229P/2 (C-21); *bottom left:* Pier 21 Society; *bottom right:* Halifax Port Corporation HPC-03; *13:* Pier 21 Society, Ted Grant collection; *14, top:* NAC PA181009; *bottom:* Pier 21 Society; *15, top:* NAC PA111579; *bottom:* Pier 21 Society; *16, left and right:* Pier 21 Society; *17, top:* Public Archives of Nova Scotia N4812-2; *bottom:* Pier 21 Society. *18, top:* Canadian National Railways 46368-1; *bottom:* Canadian National Railways 47417.5; *19, top:* Canadian National Railways X32168; *bottom:* courtesy of Devon Smiley; *inset:* Pier 21 Society; *20, top:* Public Archives of Nova Scotia PANS-419D; *bottom:* Public Archives of Nova Scotia PANS-419B; *21, top:* City of Toronto Archives 68221; *left:* Public Archives of Nova Scotia 419E; *bottom right:* City of Toronto Archives; *22, top left:* York University Archives 3398; *top right:* City of Toronto Archives 67604; *bottom:* NAC PA130032; *23:* City of Toronto Archives 68234; *24:* from *Halifax in Wartime*, courtesy of the family of Robert W. Chambers; *25, top:* Pier 21 Society; *bottom:* RCAF photograph, from the collection of the Maritime Museum of the Atlantic, Halifax, Nova Scotia MP18.141.22; *26:* NAC PA112993; *27, top:* NAC PA116510; *bottom:* Pier 21 Society; *28:* Pier 21 Society, courtesy of Flora and David Campbell; *29:* Pier 21 Society (Canadian Army); *30:* courtesy of William and Jean Sharlow; *31, top and inset:* Pier 21 Society; *bottom:* NAC PA112368; *32, top:* NAC PA175792; *bottom:* Pier 21 Society; *33, top:* courtesy of Gord Grant; *middle left and right:* Pier 21 Society; *bottom:* Pier 21 Society; *34:* Pier 21 Society; *35, top:* courtesy of Olga Raines; *bottom:* Public Archives of Nova Scotia PANS-N-4963; *36:* York University Archives #35; *37, top:* Pier 21 Society; *bottom:* Touring Club Italiano 00856710157; *38:* Pier 21 Society; *39:* Pier 21 Society; *inset:* Pier 21 Society; *40–41:* Pier 21 Society; *42, top:* author's collection; *bottom left:* courtesy of Michael Martchenko; *bottom right:* courtesy of Tundra Books; *43, top and bottom:* courtesy Michael Martchenko; *middle:* illustration by Michael Martchenko, from *High Flight: A Story of World War II*, by Linda Granfield, courtesy of Tundra Books; *44–45:* courtesy of Michael Martchenko; *46:* Pier 21 Society.